baby cr✿chet design

baby crochet design

HATS & BOOTIES

GRAZIANA MATERASSI

DOVER PUBLICATIONS, INC.
MINEOLA, NEW YORK

Dedication

To my daughters,
Kenya and Daiana, a constant source of inspiration.

Text and crochet projects by Graziana Materassi

Graphic design, lay-out, and set styling by Cinzia Chiari

Photos Archivio Giunti/Andrea Fantauzzo, Firenze

The photographer would like to thank the small models—Edward, Laura,
Leonardo, and Yoshito—for their photographic service.

Copyright

Copyright © 2014 by Giunti Editore S.p.A., Firenze—Milano
www.giunti.it

Bibliographical Note

Baby Crochet Design: Hats and Booties, first published by Dover Publications,
Inc., in 2015, was originally published in Italian as *Baby Design all'Uncinetto.
Cappellini e scarpette di cotone* by Giunti Editore S.p.A., Firenze—Milano, in 2014.

International Standard Book Number

ISBN-13: 978-0-486-79760-1
ISBN-10: 0-486-79760-0

Manufactured in the United States by RR Donnelley
79760001   2015
www.doverpublications.com

Contents

Warm weather is coming!

Now is the perfect time to think about protecting your little ones' heads from the rays of the sun, as well as from spring (and, later on, fall) winds.

There is nothing better than a hat made of pure cotton, fresh and light, whimsical and colorful, but, above all… made with your own hands! And to keep baby's little feet warm, every hat has a pair of matching booties.

It is true that some babies do not like to wear anything on their heads, but I've found that babies love colors and cute shapes: even the most anti-hat baby will want one of these! In any event, it will be a lot of fun and truly satisfying to make them yourself, choosing the color combinations that look best on your little one.

And why not make one for yourself?! Mom and Dad can show off with a hat that matches baby's!

So, yarn in one hand, crochet hook in the other, and…

Happy crocheting, and, above all, have a wonderful time!

Graziana
Nahual Artigianato Artistico, Firenze

These are patterns for stitchers who know the fundamentals of crochet: the stitches are basic, and the shapes are simple.

Make the styles your own by changing the color combinations and mixing and matching the different embellishments. Below are the abbreviations used in this book.

ABBREVIATIONS

approximately	approx	remaining	rem
begin/beginning	beg	repeat	rep
chain	ch	round	rnd
double crochet	dc	single crochet	sc
decrease	dec	single crochet 2 together	sc2tog
half double crochet	hdc	stich(es)	st(s)
increase	inc	treble crochet	tr

5-PETAL FLOWER

With size C-2 (2.75mm) hook and cotton fingering yarn, ch 4, join with sl st to form ring. **Rnd 1:** 5 sc in ring, join with sl st. **Rnd 2:** *Ch 3, (4 tr) in same st, ch 3, join with sl st in same st, sc in next sc; rep from * until you have 5 petals, join at base of first ch. For fuller petals, add 1 or 2 tr in each petal.

POINTED FLOWER

With size C-2 (2.75mm) hook and cotton fingering yarn, ch 3, join with sl st to form ring. **Rnd 1:** 5 sc in ring, join with sl st. **Rnd 2:** Ch 1, 2 sc in each sc around; join. **Rnd 3:** *Ch 3, 3 tr, ch 3, sl st in 2nd ch from hook, 2 tr, 3 ch, join with sl st in the same stitch, skip next sc, sl st in next sc; rep from * until you have 5 petals. Fasten off.

CHAIN FLOWER

With size D-3 (3.25mm) hook and cotton fingering yarn, ch 3, join with sl st to form ring. **Rnd 1:** 7 sc in ring, join with sl st. **Rnd 2:** Ch 7, *sc in next st, (ch 7, sc, ch 7) in same st; rep from * around. Join with sl st in first sc worked in. Fasten off.

FLOWER STEM

With size D-3 (3.25mm) hook and 2 strands of green cotton fingering yarn held together, ch 15. Fasten off, leaving a long tail. Make 2 knots on the end of the stem, thread it into the center of the flower and, with the knot as the pistil, use the tail to sew the stem to the flower.

OVAL LEAF

With size D-3 (3.25mm) hook and green cotton fingering yarn, ch 12. **Rnd 1:** Sc in 2nd ch from hook, sc in each ch to last ch, 3 sc in last ch, working in the other side of the ch, sc to end, join with sl st. **Rnd 2:** Ch 1, 3 sc, 2 dc, 1 tr, (2 tr) in same st, 1 tr, 2 dc, 1 sc, and (2 sc) in st at tip, 1 sc, 2 dc, 1 tr, (2 tr) in same st, 1 tr, 2 dc, 3 sc. **Next row:** Ch 12, sc in 2nd ch from hook, sc in each ch, join with sl st in first sc of rnd. Fasten off, leaving a long tail for sewing to hat.

HEART-SHAPED LEAF

With size D-3 (3.25mm) hook and green cotton fingering yarn, ch 10. **Rnd 1:** Sc in 2nd ch from hook, sc in each ch to end, 3 sc in last ch, working in opposite side of ch, sc to end, ch 1, join with sl st. **Rnd 2:** 2 sc, 2 dc,

1 tr, (2 tr) in same st, 1 tr, (3 tr) in same st, (2 tr) in same st, (1 dc, sl st) in same st, ch 1, 1 dc, (2 tr) in same st, (3 tr) in same st, 1 tr, (2 tr) in same st, 1 tr, 2 dc, 2 sc. **Rnd 3:** Ch 3, sl st in 2nd ch from hook, sl st in next ch, then continue in sc along the side of the leaf to the last 3 sts before the center, work 2 sc in each of next 3 sc, join with sl st in sl st of previous rnd. Remainder of rnd is not worked in. **Next row:** Ch 15 for the stem, sc in 2nd ch from hook, sc in each ch. Fasten off leaving a long tail for sewing.

To make a smaller leaf, use fewer sts in the foundation ch, and adjust the central stitches of the leaf. For a larger leaf, use more sts in the foundation ch, and adjust the central stitches. Work more rounds alternating rounds of sc and dc.

BRANCH WITH FLOWERS AND BERRIES

The leaf of the Mimosa hat would be a perfect starting point for a small, flowered branch.

You can easily change the length of the branch by using more or fewer chain stitches, or you can make a long branch and wind it around the hat, and embellish it with different flowers in desired colors.

Mini Flowers

To make very small flowers, you can follow the instructions of whichever flower you choose, using a finer cotton yarn and a smaller hook. You can also decrease the stitches between the petals in the next round by working sc2tog (single crochet 2 together) as follows: [insert hook in next st, yarn over hook and draw through st] twice, yarn over and draw through all 3 loops on hook.

Berries

Ch 3, join with sl st to form ring. **Rnd 1:** Work 8 sl st around ring, join with sl st. Fasten off, leaving a long tail. With the tapestry needle, thread the tail through the foundation ch to form a ball. Make as many little balls as you need.

Finishing

Place the branch on the hat and arrange it as you desire. With the tapestry needle and the same yarn as the berries, sew the berries onto the twig. It isn't necessary to sew the leaf onto the hat; it is enough to fasten it with the berries.

BUTTERFLY

The butterfly works well for either a boy's or a girl's hat.

Body

With size C-2 (2.25mm) hook and cotton fingering yarn in purple, ch 15. **Rnd 1:** Sc in 2nd ch from hook, sc in each ch to last ch, (5 sc) in same ch for the butterfly's head, work 1 sc in each st on the other side of the foundation ch to end, ch 4, sl st in 2nd ch from hook, sl st in next 2 ch, join to beg of rnd with sl st. Fasten off.

Wing Centers

Join orange yarn in the 4th st after the butterfly's head, sc in same st as joining, ch 6, sc in 2nd ch from hook and in each following ch, join to base with sc. Fasten off. Repeat on the other side of the head. Start working again in the 4th st after the orange cord towards the tail. Make this in the same way as the other cords, but with ch 4 instead of 6. Rep on the other side.

Large Wings

With yellow yarn, start working from the base of one of the orange cords near the head. Make 1 sc in the purple stitch near the cord and work your way up the cord with 1 sc, 1 tr, (2 tr) in the same st, (2 tr) in the next st, (4 tr) in the next st; working on the opposite side of the cord, work (4 tr) in next st, (2 tr) in next st, (2 tr) in next st, 1 tr, 1 sc. Rep on opposite side for other wing.

Small Wings

Work as for large wing, working 2 less tr on the sides of each wing. With the purple yarn, work 1 rnd sc around the 4 wings, working 3 inc in the curve of each wing.

Antennae

With orange yarn, ch 10 and fasten off. Pass the cord through the butterfly's head, and make a small knot on each end.

Not Only For Babies: Caps Made to Measure

When worked in cotton fingering yarn at a gauge of 22 sts and 26 rnds to 4in./10cm the instructions will yield a hat to fit size 1 for a 3-8 month old baby. For babies from newborn to 2 months, follow the instructions as written using thinner cotton and a smaller hook for a gauge of 26 sts to 4in./10cm: the styles will "automatically" be the right size.

The table below indicates how to make styles adapted for children up to 3 years old, as well as for other age groups. Age and head circumference size will help you to find the right measurements for your hat. The larger sizes should be worked in cotton fingering yarn at a gauge of 18 sts and 26 rnds to 4in./10cm.

Hats

Crochet has elasticity and cotton won't shrink as long as it isn't washed in hot water. With use and washing it tends to stretch. Therefore, keep in mind that a hat for a 1 year old will also be able to be worn by a 2 year old.

Booties

Only a baby who is not yet walking can wear crocheted booties. The instructions are for children at least 3 months old; for smaller babies, use thinner cotton and a smaller hook.

Details

Follow the directions as written for sizes 1 and 2. For all the ears, the frog's eyes, and the piggy's nose, to make sizes 3 and 4 add 2 stitches. For the owl's eyes, add 1 round to the pupils and increase 3 stitches evenly in the round. For the rooster's crest, add 6 chains to the foundation chain and you will have 2 more points; for the beak, add 2 chains to the foundation chain and you will have 1 more round.

SIZE	AGE	STITCHES	ROUNDS IN THE CIRCUMFERENCE	HEAD CIRCUMFERENCE	HAT LENGTH
1	8-12 months	77	33	14in./36cm	5in./13cm
2	2	82	36	18in./45cm	5½in./14cm
3	3	87	39	19¾in./50cm	6in./15cm
4	4	92	42	20½in./52cm	6½in./16cm
	5 years–Adult	97	45	21½–23in./55–58cm	7in./18cm

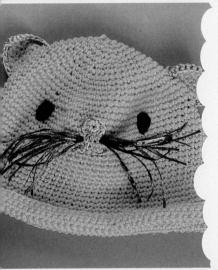

The Projects

Cute little animals, magical elves, colorful fruit…
what strikes your fancy today?!

Red Like a Strawberry

What does Little Red Riding Hood collect
in the forest to take to her grandmother?
Perhaps a lot of sweet strawberries. . .

MATERIALS

For the hat: 3½oz/100g of cotton fingering yarn in red, 1¾oz/50g of acid green, small
amount of black cotton yarn, size D-3 (3.25mm) crochet hook, tapestry needle.

For the booties: 1¾oz/50g of cotton fingering yarn in red, small amounts of acid green,
black, white, and yellow, size D-3 (3.25mm) crochet hook, stitch markers, tapestry needle.

Red Like a Strawberry

HAT

With the red cotton, ch 4, join with sl st to form ring.

Rnd 1: Work 9 sc in ring.

Rnd 2: *Sc in sc, 2 sc in next sc; rep from * around working 2 sc in last sc—14 sc.

Rnd 3: *Sc in sc, 2 sc in next sc; rep from * around—21 sc.

Rnd 4: *Sc in next 3 sc, 2 sc in next sc; rep from * around, sc in last sc.

Rnds 5 and 6: *Sc in next 5 sc, 2 sc in next st; rep from * around, sc to end of rnd.

Rnds 7–12: Sc, inc 5 sts evenly around by working (2 sc) in same st—65 sc at end of rnd 12.

Rnd 13: Sc, inc 7 sts evenly around—72 sc.

Rnds 14–33: Sc in each sc around.

Rnd 34: This is the last round before starting the brim. Hold the yarn tighter than for previous rounds so the hat does not flare.

Starting the Brim

Rnd 1: *Sc in next 3 sc, 2 sc in next sc; rep from * around—90 sc.

Rnd 2: Work even.

Rnd 3: *Sc in next 7 sc, 2 sc in next sc, sc in 6 sc, 2 sc in next sc; rep from * around—102 sc.

Rnds 4 and 5: Sc in each sc around.

Last Round (Fan Stitch)

*Skip 2 sc, (6 tr) in next sc, skip 2 sc, sl st in next sc; rep from * around. Fasten off.

Stem and Leaves

With 2 strands of green held together, ch 7.

Stem row: Beg in 2nd ch from hook, sc in each ch to the last st, cut 1 strand and cont with 1 strand only, work (6 sc) in last ch, join with sl st to form a ring of these 6 sc. Work leaves in the sts of the ring formed by the last 6 sc as follows:

Rnd 1: Holding the stem to the front, *2 sc in next sc; rep from * around—12 sc.

Rnd 2: *Sc in next 1 sc, 2 sc in next sc; rep from * around—18 sc.

Rnds 3 and 4: *Sc in next 2 sc, 2 sc in next sc; rep from * around, sc to end—32 sc.

Rnds 5 and 6: *Sc inc 8 sts evenly around— 48 sts.

Last rnd: Work in fan st as for hat edge.

Finishing

Sew the leaves to the hat, matching the stem with the center of the hat. Sew last rnd of sc to the hat, leaving the fan stitches free.

With the tapestry needle and the black yarn, embroider black dots onto the hat, using the photo as a guide. If you prefer, you can embroider the dots with white cotton.

BOOTIES

With 2 strands of red held together, ch 10. Cut 1 strand and continue with 1 strand only.

Rnd 1: Sc in 2nd ch from hook, sc in each ch to last, (3 sc) in last ch, place marker in 2nd sc of the 3, sc in opposite side of next ch, sc in each ch to last ch, 2 sc in last ch, place marker in last sc—20 sc.

Rnds 2 and 3: [Sc in each sc to marked sc, (3 sc) in marked sc, move marker to 2nd sc of the 3] twice—28 sc.

Rnd 4: [Sc in next 6 sc, (2 sc) in next sc, sc to marked sc, (3 sc) in marked sc, move marker up] twice—34 sc.

Rnd 5: [Sc in each sc to 1 sc before marker, 2 sc in next sc, 3 sc in marked sc, move marker up, 2 sc in next sc] twice—42 sc.

Rnds 6–9: Sc in each sc, moving marker up. Do not increase.

Rnd 10: [Sc in each sc to 1 st before marked st, sc2tog] twice—40 sc.

Rnd 11: Sc in each sc.

Fold the bootie lengthwise and flatten it to find the center between the ends, place a marker in each center st; sc to first marker, ch 8, join with sc in opposite marker, turn, and work in sc to beg of ch 8, sc in each ch, continue to work around to beg of rnd, sl st in next sc. Fasten off. This forms the cuff.

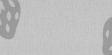

Red Like a Strawberry

Upper

Row 1: Join yarn at base of ch 8, work 8 sc in opposite side of ch 8, ch 1, turn.

Rows 2–5: (2 sc) in same sc as turning ch, sc to last sc, (2 sc) in last sc, ch 1, turn.

Row 6: Sc in each sc across, ch 1, turn.

Rows 7–9: Sc2tog, sc to last 2 sc, sc2tog, ch 1, turn. Fasten off, leaving a long tail for sewing later.

Cuff Edging

With green yarn, work 1 rnd sc around edge of the cuff of the bootie, join with sl st.

Turn the bootie inside out and work in fan stitch as for the hat, working 7 tr for each fan.

Drawstring

With 2 strands of green yarn held together, make a chain 20in./50cm long. Fasten off.

Flowerets

With yellow yarn, ch 4, join with sl st to form ring.

Rnd 1: Work 10 sc in ring, join with sl st. Fasten off.

Rnd 2: Join white yarn in any st, *1 sc, in next sc, (ch 3, 5 tr, ch 3, sc); rep from * 4 times more—5 petals. Fasten off.

Finishing

Turn the bootie right side out. With the tapestry needle and the tail of yarn, sew the upper to the corresponding edge of the bootie.

Weave the drawstring through the sts 2 rnds below the fan stitch leaves, ending with both ends of the drawstrings at the front; pass the ends through the center of the floweret. Tighten and loosen the bootie around the ankle by sliding the drawstring up and down through the floweret. Tie a knot at each end of the drawstring to keep the floweret secure.

With the tapestry needle and black or white yarn (depending on the color chosen for the hat), embroider the strawberry dots on the booties.

Make a 2nd bootie same as the first.

The Wide-mouthed Frog

Turn your little prince or princess
into a kissable frog.

MATERIALS

For the hat: 1³/₄oz/50g of cotton fingering yarn in acid green, small amounts of white, black, orange, and red, size D-3 (3.25mm) crochet hook, tapestry needle, stitch markers.

For the booties: 1³/₄oz/50g of cotton fingering yarn in acid green, small amounts of white, black, orange, and red, size D-3 (3.25mm) crochet hook, tapestry needle.

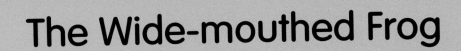

The Wide-mouthed Frog

HAT

Work as for the strawberry hat to the brim.

Brim

Rnd 1: *Sc in next 3 sc, 2 sc in next sc; rep from * around—90 sc.

Rnd 2: Sc in each sc around.

Rnd 3: *Sc in next 8 sc, 2 sc in next sc; rep from * around—100 sc.

Rnd 4–7: Sc in each sc around.

Rnd 8: *Sc in next 9 sc, 2 sc in next sc; rep from * around—110 sc.

Rnd 9: Sc in each sc around.

Rnd 10: Work 1 rnd of sl st very tightly around to give the hat its shape. Fasten off.

Outer Eyes

Flatten the hat to find the midpoint on the front. Place a marker at the center brim and on the sides 16 rounds down from the top of the hat. Join the acid green yarn in 1 marked side st, leaving a tail approximately 8in./20cm long.

Row 1: Working toward the top of the hat, sc in marked rnd and in each of next 5 rnds, ch 1. Turn.

Row 2: (2 sc) in first sc, sc in each sc to last sc, (2 sc) in last sc, ch 1. Turn.

Row 3: (2 sc) in first sc, sc in 2 sc, (2 sc) in next sc, sc to last st, (2 sc) in last sc, ch 1. Turn.

Rows 4–7: Sc in each sc to end, ch 1, turn.

Rows 8 and 9: Sc2tog, sc in each sc to last 2 sts, skip 1 sc, sc in last sc, ch 1. Turn.

Row 10: Sc2tog, sc to last st, sc along edge of eye to the hat.

Row 11: Holding the beginning tail along the edge of the outer eye, work in reverse single crochet around the edge of the eye and the beginning tail. Fasten off.

Rep for the 2nd outer eye, working in the opposite marked side st.

Eyes

(Make 2)

With black yarn, ch 4, join with sl st to form ring.

Rnd 1: Work 10 sc in ring.

Rnd 2: *Sc in next sc, (3 sc) in next sc; rep from * around—20 sc.

Rnd 3: Sc in next 2 sc, (2 sc) in next sc; rep from * around—26 sc. Fasten off.

Rnd 4: Join white yarn, work 1 sc in each sc around.

Rnd 5: Sc in each sc around.

Rnd 6: Sc in next 2 sc, skip 1; rep from * around, join with sl st—18 sc. Fasten off, leaving a long tail.

Tongue

With the red yarn, ch 10.

Rnd 1: Sc in 2nd ch from hook, and in each ch to last ch, (3 sc) in last ch, place marker in 2nd sc, working in opposite side of foundation chain, skipping the ch with the increases, sc to last ch, (3 sc) in last ch, place marker in 2nd sc.

Rnds 2 and 3: [Sc to marked st, (3 sc) in marked st, move marker up] twice. Fasten off, leaving a long tail.

Finishing

Stuff the black portion of each eye with black yarn, using enough material so that it will keep its shape.

Position the eye in the center of the outer eye and gently pull the green tail that is under the reverse single crochet to cup the outer eye around the eye. With the tapestry needle, fasten the tail very securely on the reverse side. Sew in the eye, fastening it inside the outer eye at the base of the reverse single crochet. Be sure that the eye maintains its shape as you sew. Fasten both ends securely on the reverse side. Rep for 2nd eye.

With the tapestry needle and the orange yarn, embroider a wide mouth in a half-moon shape, using chain st. Use tail to sew the tongue to the left or to the right of the frog's mouth, with the tip towards the eyes. Leave the lower part of the tongue free so that it curls.

The Wide-mouthed Frog

BOOTIES

Work same as the strawberry booties, working 1 rnd in reverse single crochet with orange, instead of the fan stitch leaves.

Eyes

(Make 2 for each bootie)

With the black yarn, ch 4, join with sl st to form ring.

Rnd 1: 10 sc in the ring. Fasten off, leaving a long tail for sewing.

Rnd 2: With the white yarn, [sc in next 2 sc, (2 sc) in next sc] 3 times, sc in last sc. Fasten off.

Tongue

(Make 1 for each bootie)

With the red yarn, ch 6. Sc in 2nd ch from hook, sc in each ch to last, (3 sc) in last ch, sc in the opposite side of foundation ch to the last st, (3 sc) in last ch. Fasten off, leaving a long tail for sewing.

Finishing

Sew on the eyes using the photo as a guide.

With the tapestry needle and the orange yarn, using chain st, embroider a mouth in a half-moon shape. Sew the frog's tongue to the right side of the mouth; on the other bootie, sew it to the left side so that they mirror each other.

Drawstring

(Make 1 for each bootie)

With 2 strands of green yarn held together, make a chain 20in./50cm long. Fasten off. Weave the drawstring from the inside to the outside every 4–5 sts around the ankle, leaving the ends free at the back.

Button

(Make 1 for each bootie)

Ch 4, join with sl st to form ring. Work 10 sc in ring. Fasten off. Weave tail into ring.

Pass the ends of the drawstring through the hole of the button. Slide the button to tighten and loosen the bootie. Make a knot on each end of the drawstring.

It's Snack Time: How About a Refreshing Pineapple?

You don't need to be on vacation in the tropics to be keen on this hat, which is zesty and delicious just like your little one.

MATERIALS

For the hat: 3½oz/100g of cotton fingering yarn in lemon yellow, 1¾oz/50g in olive green, size D-3 (3.25mm) crochet hook, tapestry needle, stitch markers.

For the booties: 1¾oz/50g of cotton fingering yarn in lemon yellow, small amount in olive green, size D-3 (3.25mm) crochet hook, yellow (or transparent) elastic thread.

Refreshing Pineapple

HAT

With the yellow yarn, ch 4, join with sl st to form ring. Work 12 sc into ring.

Rnd 1: *Sc in next sc, (2 sc) in next sc; rep from * around. Place last st on safety pin to hold. Drop but do not cut the yellow yarn.

Rnd 2: Join the olive green yarn with sl st in first sc, sc in same st as joining, *ch 2, skip next 2 sc, sc in next sc; rep from * around. Drop the green yarn, and place last st on a safety pin to hold.

Rnd 3: Holding green sts to the front, with yellow, work into the sts of rnd 1 as follows: *(2 sc) in each of next 2 sc, skip green sc; rep from * around. Place last st on safety pin to hold.

Rnd 4: With green, *ch 2, skip next 2 sc, sc in next sc; rep from * around. Fasten off the green yarn.

Rnd 5: With yellow, work as for rnd 3—30 sc.

Rnd 6: *Sc in next 4 sc, (2 sc) in next sc; rep from * around—36 sc.

Rnd 7: *Sc in next 8 sc, (2 sc) in next sc; rep from * around—40 sc.

Solid Scallop Stitch

Rnd 1: Ch 1, *skip 1 sc, (6 tr) in next sc (scallop made); skip next sc, sc in next sc; rep from * around, join with sl st in beg ch 1.

Rnds 2–3: Ch 3, *sc in center of next scallop, make scallop in next sc; rep from * around. Work last scallop in the base of the beg ch 3, sk ch 3, sl st in next sc.

Rnd 4–11: Rep rnd 2, making scallops with 7 tr instead of 6.

Rnd 12: Continue in pattern, making scallops with 6 tr.

Rnd 13: Sc in same st as sl st; sc in next sc and in each st around—70 sc.

Rnd 14: *Sc in next 2 sc, (2 sc) in next sc; rep from * around, sc to end—93 sc.

Rnd 15: Sc in each sc around.

Rnd 16: *Sc in next 8 sc, (2 sc) in next sc; rep from * around, sc to end—103 sc.

Rnd 17: Sc around, sl st in first sc of rnd.

Fan stitch edge: Skip 2 sc, (6 tr) in next sc, skip 2 sc, sc in next sc; rep from * around, ending with sl st in first sl st. Fasten off.

Leaves

The leaves are worked into the green rounds at the top of the hat.

Rnd 1: Join the green yarn in the first ch-2 space in the green ring closest to top of hat, ch 1, *2 sc in chain-2 space, sc in next sc; rep from * around, join with sl st to beg ch 1—15sc.

Rnd 2: Sc in next 2 sc, *ch 9, sc in 2nd ch from hook, sc in next 2 sc, dc in next 5 dc, skip 2 sc, sc in next sc; rep from * for 5 half-leaves; join with sl st.

Rnd 3: Working into the opposite side of the ch of 1 half-leaf, *dc in next 5 ch, sc in next 3 ch, ch 3, sl st in 2nd ch from hook, sc in each st to base of leaf, rep from *, working in opposite side of ch of each half-leaf around. Fasten off.

Work the 2nd layer of leaves into the 2nd green ring in the same way, working ch 11 for each half-leaf and using 7 dc instead of 5.

Finishing

If needed, tack the leaves to the top of the hat, being sure that the tips of the leaves are free.

BOOTIES

With 2 strands of yellow held together, ch 10. Cut 1 strand of yarn and continue with a single strand of yarn.

Rnds 1–7: Work same as for strawberry booties.

Refreshing Pineapple

Rnd 8: [Sc in each sc to 1 st before marked st, sc2tog] twice—40 sc.

Rnd 9: Work in solid scallop pattern as for hat.

Rnd 10: Continue in scallop pattern.

Rnds 11 and 12: Continue in pattern working scallops with 5 tr instead of 6 tr.

Rnd 13: Work around in sc, join with sl st at end of rnd—60 sc.

CAREFUL: Do not cut the yarn!

Fold and flatten the bootie lengthwise. The portion further away from the end of the last rnd will be the toe of the bootie.

With the tapestry needle and yellow yarn, start to stitch from the toe of the bootie to the end of the 2nd scallop.

Measure a length of elastic to the same measurement as the circumference of the opening of the bootie. Make a tight knot and cut it leaving a tail 1in./2cm long.

Rnd 14: Place the loop of yarn from rnd 13 on the hook. Keeping the knot at the back and being sure that the elastic is on the inside, work over the elastic as follows: *sc in next 4 sc, sc next 2 sc together; rep from * around, sc to end.

Leaves

Turn the bootie inside out.

Rnd 1: Join the green yarn to the back of the bootie, *sc in 2 sc, (ch 7, sc in 3rd ch from hook, sc in next 2 ch, dc in next 2 ch, tr in next ch, skip next 2 sc of bootie; rep from * around, sl st in first sc of rnd. You may need to skip 1 more or less sts at the end of the rnd. You should have 8 or 9 half leaves

Rnd 2: *Working up opposite side of ch-7 of next half leaf, tr in next ch, dc in next 2 ch, sc in next 3 ch, ch 3, sl st in 2nd ch from hook, sc in each of next 6 sts, sl st between leaves; rep from * around. Fasten off.

Make a 2nd bootie same as the first.

The Elf of Our Dreams

The perfect set for a baby who is mischievous and magical like an elf in a fairy tale!

MATERIALS

For the hat: 3¹/₂oz/100g of cotton fingering yarn in purple, small amounts of orange, yellow, pink, and green for the flowers, sizes D-3 and C-2 (3.25mm and 2.75mm) crochet hooks, tapestry needle, stitch markers.

For the booties: 1³/₄oz/50g of cotton fingering yarn in purple, small amounts of orange, yellow, pink and green, size D-3 (3.25mm) crochet hook, tapestry needle.

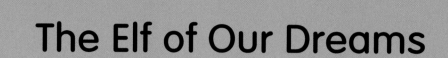

The Elf of Our Dreams

HAT

With 2 strands of purple yarn held together, ch 8.

Rnd 1: Sl st in 2nd ch from hook, sl st in next 2 ch, sc in next 4 ch. Cut one strand and continue working with one strand only.

Rnd 2: Insert hook in opposite side of ch, (6 sc) in same ch, holding the chain to the front, join with 1 sl st in 1st sc. Work hat in ring formed by the 6 sc.

Rnd 3: *Sc in next 2 sc, (2 sc) in next sc; rep from * around—8 sc.

Rnd 4: *Sc in next 3 sc, (2 sc) in next sc; rep from * around—10 sc.

Rnds 5 and 6: Sc in each sc around.

Rnd 7: *Sc in next 4 sc, (2 sc) in next sc; rep from * around—12 sc.

Rnd 8: *Sc in next 3 sc, (2 sc) in next sc; rep from * around—15 sc.

Rnd 9–16: Sc in each sc around.

Rnd 17: Sc in next 5 sc, (2 sc) in next sc; rep from * around, sc to end—17 sc.

Rnds 18–21: *Sc in next 4 sc, (2 sc) in next sc; rep from * around, sc to end—33 sc.

Rnds 22–28: Work in sc, inc 5 sts evenly around by (2 sc) in same sc—68 sc.

Rnd 29: Work in sc, inc 9 sts evenly around by (2 sc) in same sc. Be sure that you have 77 sc at the end of this rnd.

Work 4 rnds even in sc.

Brim

Rnd 1: *Sc in next 2 sc (2 sc) in next sc; rep from * around, sc to end.

Rnd 2: Sc in each sc around.

Rnd 3: *Sc in next 8 sc, (2 sc) in next sc; rep from *, sc to end.

Rnds 4 and 5: Sc in each sc around.

Rnd 6: Sl st tightly in each sc around. Fasten off.

Embellish the hat as in the photo by adding flowers following the directions given in the beginning of the book. If the hat is for a boy, you might add a yellow ladybug or some leaves instead of the flowers.

BOOTIES

With the purple yarn, work rows 1–11 as for the strawberry booties.

Flatten the bootie lengthwise, find the center of each side. With the tapestry needle and the purple yarn, seam the front of the bootie by sewing the top edge together from the halfway mark to the toe.

Cuff

Row 1: Join yarn 2 sts after the seam, work in sc to 2 sts before the seam, ch 1. Turn.

Row 2: (2 sc) in next sc, *sc in next 3 sc, (2 sc) in next st; rep from * once, sc to end, working (2 sc) in last sc, ch 1. Turn.

Row 3: Rep rnd 2.

Row 4: (2 sc) in first sc, sc in each sc to last sc, (2 sc) in last sc, ch 1. Turn.

Row 5: (2 sc) in first sc, sc in each sc to last sc, (2 sc) in last sc, ch 1. Turn.

Row 6: Sl st in each st to end of row. Fasten off.

Make a 2nd bootie same as the first.

Finishing

With 2 strands of green yarn held together, make 2 drawstrings of 60 ch each.

Weave a drawstring in and out of row 1 of each cuff, finishing with both ends outside and in the front.

Make 4 small flowers of your choice following the directions in the beginning of the book, and attach them to the ends of the drawstrings. Knot the ends of drawstrings to keep the flowers in place.

Lily of the Valley— With a Touch of Red

Gnomes, fairies, and squirrels! All the creatures of the forest meet under this hat: we are ready for a picnic.

MATERIALS

For the hat: 3½oz/100g of cotton fingering yarn in white, 1¾oz/50g in green, small amounts of red and black, sizes C-2 and D-3 (2.75 and 3.25mm) crochet hooks, tapestry needle, stitch markers.

For the booties: 1¾oz/50g of cotton fingering yarn in white, 1½oz/50g in green, and small amounts of red and black, size D-3 (3.25mm) crochet hook, tapestry needle.

Lily of the Valley

HAT

Work as for the Strawberry hat to the last round before the brim—72 sc.

Brim

Rnd 1: *Sc in next 2 sc, (2 sc) in next sc; rep from * around—96 sc.

Rnd 2: Sc in each sc around.

Rnd 3: *Sc in next 9 sc, (2 sc) in next sc; rep from * around, sc to end—105 sc.

Rnd 4: Sc in each sc around.

Rnd 5: [Sc in next 20 sc, 2 dc in next sc] 5 times around—110 sc.

Rnd 6: [Sc in next 20 sc, dc in next 2 dc] 5 times around—130 sc.

Rnd 7: [Sl st in next 20 sc, ch 2, sl st in first ch, skip 2 dc] 5 times around, join with sl st. Fasten off.

Ladybug

With the red yarn and the smaller hook, ch 6.

Rnd 1: (2 sc) in 2nd ch from hook, place a marker in first sc, sc in each ch to end, (3 sc) in last ch, place a marker in 2nd sc made,

working in opposite side of ch, skip the last ch, work in each ch to end.

Rnd 2: [Sc to marked st, (3 sc) in marked sc, move marker to center st] twice, sc to end.

Rnds 3 and 4: [Sc to marked st, (3 sc) in marked sc, move marker to center st, sc in each st to the middle of the side, (2 sc) in same st] twice, sc to end.

Rnd 5: Sl st tightly in each sc around. Fasten off.

Ladybug Antennae

With the black yarn and the smaller hook, count 4 sts to the right from the first marked st. Join with sl st, and working in rnd of sc below the last sl st rnd, sc in same st as joining, ch 8, (4 sc) in 2nd ch from hook, sc in each ch to end, sc in next st along ladybug edge, (2 sc) in next st, sc in next st, ch 8, (4 sc) in 2nd ch from hook, sc in each ch to end, sc in next st along ladybug edge. Fasten off, leaving a long tail.

Thread the tail through the tapestry needle and embroider 3 black dots on each side of the ladybug, using the photo as a guide.

Set the ladybug aside.

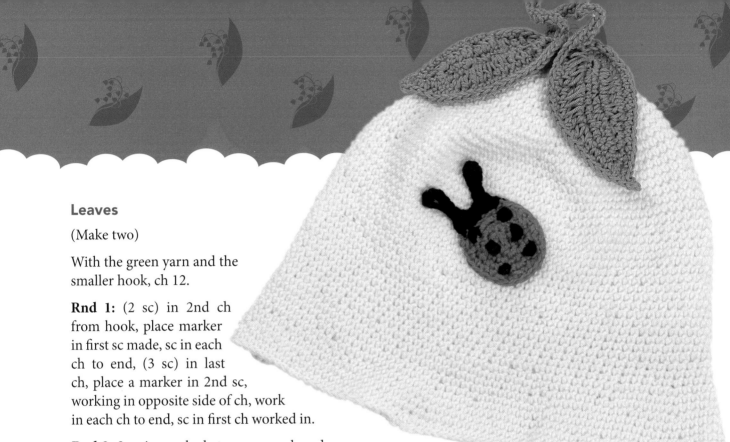

Leaves

(Make two)

With the green yarn and the smaller hook, ch 12.

Rnd 1: (2 sc) in 2nd ch from hook, place marker in first sc made, sc in each ch to end, (3 sc) in last ch, place a marker in 2nd sc, working in opposite side of ch, work in each ch to end, sc in first ch worked in.

Rnd 2: 3 sc in marked st, move marker, dc in next sc, tr in 2 sc, (2 tr) in next sc, tr in 2 sc, dc in 3 sc, sc in 2 sc, 3 sc in marked st, move marker, sc in 2 sc, dc in 3 sc, tr in 2 sc, (2 tr) in next sc, tr in 2 sc, dc in next sc, sc in next sc.

Rnd 3: 3 sc in marked st, move marker, sc in 3 sts, (2 sc) in next st, sc in each st to marked st, (2 sc) in next st, ch 3, sl st in 2nd ch from hook, sc in next ch, sc in 10 sts, (2 sc) in next st, sc to end.

Rnd 4: Ch 15 for stem, sc in 2nd ch from hook, sc in each ch, sl st in each st to tip of leaf, ch 3, sl st in 2nd ch from hook, sl st in next ch, sl st around leaf to stem. Fasten off.

Finishing

Sew the leaves to the top of the hat, leaving the tips free.

Sew the ladybug to the hat, using the photo as a guide.

BOOTIES

Work as for the strawberry booties, through the upper.

Cuff

Row 1: Join yarn in the 6th st to the left from the upper, sc in each st to 5 sts before

37

Lily of the Valley

opposite end of upper, ch 1. Turn.

Rows 2 and 3: Sc in each sc to end, ch 1. Turn.

Row 4: Sc in each sc to end, ch 3, sc in base of ch. Turn.

Row 5: Work 4 sc in the chain-3 space, sc in each sc to end of row, ch 3, sl st in base of chain to form ring, 4 sc in ring, sl st in base of ring. Fasten off.

Ladybugs

With the red yarn and the smaller hook, ch 4.

Rnd 1: (2 sc) in 2nd ch from hook, place a marker in first sc, sc in each ch to end, (3 sc) in last ch, place a marker in center sc, skipping ch just worked, sc in opposite side of ch to end.

Rnds 2 and 3: Sc to marked st, (2 sc) in marked st, inc in center of row by (2 sc) in same st] twice, sc to end. Fasten off.

Join the black yarn 1 st to the right of one marked st, sc in same st as joining, ch 4.

Rnd 4: 4 sc in 2nd from hook, sl st in each ch to base, (2 sc) in next 2 sc along edge of ladybug, ch 4, sc in 2nd from hook, sl st in each ch to base, sc in edge of ladybug. Fasten off, leaving a long tail.

Thread tail through tapestry needle and embroider 6 black dots on the ladybug's body, using the photo as a guide.

Laces

With 2 strands of green yarn held together, ch 60. Fasten off.

Finishing

Sew the ladybugs to the booties using the photo as a guide.

Sew the upper to the sole.

Pass the lace through the loops (see photo), and make a knot at each end.

Make a 2nd bootie same as the first.

Green Apple with a Red Caterpillar

This fresh, crisp apple brings along
a cheery friend for baby.

MATERIALS

For the hat: 3½oz/100g of cotton fingering yarn in acid green, small amounts of olive green, red, and yellow, sizes B-1, C-2, and D-3 (2.25, 2.75, and 3.25mm) crochet hooks, tapestry needle, stitch markers.

For the booties: 1¾oz/50g of cotton fingering yarn in acid green, small amounts of olive green, red, and yellow, C-2 and D-3 (2.75 and 3.25mm) crochet hooks, tapestry needle.

Green Apple with a Red Caterpillar

HAT

With the acid green yarn, work as for the frog hat through the brim.

Leaves

With the olive green cotton yarn, make 2 leaves as for the lily of the valley hat.

Caterpillar

The caterpillar is made up of 5 disks.

1ST DISK (TAIL)

With the red yarn and the B-2 (2.25mm) hook, ch 4, join with a sl st, to form ring.

Rnd 1: 8 sc in ring.

Rnd 2: *Sc in next sc, (2 sc) in next sc; rep

from * around, join with sl st, ch 1. Turn.

Rnd 3: Sc in next 4 sc, ch 1. Turn.

Rnd 4: [Sc2tog] twice, ch 3, sl st in 2nd ch from hook, sl st in next ch, sc in next 2 sc, join to base of disk with sl st. Fasten off.

2ND DISK

Ch 2, join with sl st to form ring.

Rnd 1: Work 8 sc in ring.

Rnd 2: *Sc in next sc, (2 sc) in next sc; rep from * around.

Rnd 3: Rep rnd 2.

Rnd 4: *Sc in next 2 sc, (2 sc) in next sc. Fasten off leaving a long tail.

3RD AND 4TH DISKS

Work as for 2nd disc.

5TH DISK (FACE)

Work as for 2nd disk through rnd 4.

Rnd 5: *Sc in next 3 sc, (2 sc) in next sc; rep from * around. Fasten off, leaving a long tail.

Rnd 6: Join the yellow yarn in any st, sc in same st as joining, sc in next st, ch 8, (4 sc) in 2nd ch from hook, sl st in each ch to base,

sc in next 4 sts in edge of disk, ch 8, (4 sc) in 2nd ch from hook, sl st in each ch to base, sc in next 2 sc. Fasten off, leaving a long tail.

With the yellow yarn, embroider 2 small eyes and a small half-moon smile on the caterpillar's little face, using the photo as a guide.

Finishing

Sew the leaves to the top of the hat, leaving the stems free. Attach the stems in the center and leave the leaf tip free, so that it curls up a little.

Arrange the discs on the hat to form a caterpillar as follows:

Sew on the disc for the tail, attaching it along the last round. Then, place the 2nd disc on top of it, without covering the center of the tail disk, and sew it on with the tail of yarn. Attach the remaining disks in the same way.

Arrange the caterpillar on the hat as desired. Note that you can make the caterpillar longer by adding disks.

BOOTIES

With the acid green yarn and the D-3 (3.25 mm) hook, work as for the frog booties without sewing the upper to the sole.

With the olive green yarn, start working from the back of the last rnd of the cuff and work 1 rnd sc, inc 4 sts evenly around by (2 sc) in the same st. Work 1 rnd of reverse single crochet.

Make a 2nd bootie same as the first.

Green Apple with a Red Caterpillar

Make 2 drawstrings as follows: With 2 strands of olive green yarn held together, ch 60 and fasten off.

Small Caterpillar

The small caterpillar for the booties is made up of 4 small disks.

1ST DISK (TAIL)

With the red yarn and the C-2 (2.25mm) hook, ch 4 and join with sl st to form ring.

Rnd 1: Work 8 sc in ring, ch 1. Turn.

Rnd 2: Sc in next sc, ch 2, sl st in 2nd ch from hook, join to base of disk with a sl st. Fasten off, leaving a long tail.

2ND AND 3RD DISKS (BODY)

Ch 4 and join with sl st to form ring.

Rnd 1: Work 8 sc in ring.

Rnd 2: *Sc in next sc, (2 sc) in next 2 sc; rep from * around.

Rnd 3: *Sc in next 2 sc, (2 sc) in next sc; rep from * around. Fasten off.

4TH DISK (FACE)

Work rnds 1–3 as for 2nd disk, then rep rnd 3 once more. Fasten off.

ANTENNAE

Join the yellow yarn with a sl st anywhere on 4th disk, sc in same st as joining, ch 4, work (3 sc) in 2nd ch from hook, sl st in next 2 ch, sc in base of ch, sc in next 2 sc along edge of disk, ch 4, work (3 sc) in 2nd ch from hook, sl st in next 2 ch, sc in base of ch. Fasten off.

With the tapestry needle and the tail of yellow yarn, embroider 2 small eyes and a small half-moon mouth, using the photo as a guide.

Finishing

With the tapestry needle and the green yarn, working on the right side, sew the upper to the sole.

Sew the tail disk and the 2nd disk to the right bootie so that the 2nd disk doesn't cover the center of the tail disk. On the bootie for the left foot, first sew the 3rd disk and then the caterpillar's face, using the photo as a guide.

Weave the drawstring into the bootie every 3 sts, working 4 rnds below the top edge, leaving the ends free towards the front. Make a knot on each end.

Lucky Ladybug

Who stole the ladybug's spots?
It seems that they all ended up on this hat…
and with matching sandals, flying almost
seems possible!

MATERIALS

For the hat: 1³/₄oz/50g of cotton fingering yarn in red, small amounts of black and turquoise, sizes C-2 and D-3 (2.25 and 3.25mm) crochet hooks, tapestry needle, stitch markers, straight pins to hold the decorations when finishing.

For the booties: 1³/₄oz/50g of cotton fingering yarn in red, small amounts of black and turquoise, sizes C-2 and D-3 (2.25 and 3.25mm) crochet hooks, tapestry needle.

46

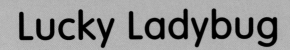

Lucky Ladybug

HAT

With the red yarn and the larger hook, work as for the frog hat through the brim.

Face

With the black yarn and the larger hook, ch 7.

Rnd 1: Sc in 2nd ch from hook and in each ch to end, (3 sc) in last ch, place marker in center sc, working in opposite side of ch, sc in next sc, sc in each ch to end, (2 sc) in first ch, place marker in last sc.

Rnd 2: [Sc in each sc to 1 st before marked st, (2 sc) in next sc, mark first sc, sc in marked st of previous rnd, removing marker, (2 sc) in next sc, mark last sc] twice.

Rnds 3 and 4: [Sc in each sc to marked st, 2 sc in marked st, move marker up to first sc made, sc to marked st, (2 sc) in marked st, move marker to last st made] 2 times to form a rectangle.

Rnd 5: [Sc in each sc to marked st, sc in marked st, remove marker, (3 sc) in next st, sc to 1 st before next marked st, (3 sc) in next st, sc in marked st, remove marker] twice,

ch 10, (4 hdc) in 3rd ch from hook, hdc in each ch to base of ch, sl st in base of ch and in next sc, sc in 4 sc; rep from * to *. Fasten off.

Nose

With the red yarn and C-2 (2.75mm) hook, ch 3, join with sl st to form ring. Fasten off, leaving a long tail. Thread the tail through the tapestry needle, and draw the sts together to form a small ball. Secure the yarn and cut the tail.

Small Spots

(Make 4)

With the black yarn and the B-1 (2.25mm) hook, ch 3, join with sl st to form ring.

Rnd 1: Work 8 sc in ring.

Rnd 2: (2 sc) in each sc around.

Rnd 3: *Sc in next sc, (2 sc) in next sc; rep from * around. Join with sl st and fasten off, leaving a long tail.

Large Spot

(Make 2)

Work same as small spot through rnd 3.

Rnds 3–5: *Sc in next 2 sc, (2 sc) in next sc; rep from * around, sc to end. Join with sl st and fasten off.

Cord

With 2 strands of yarn held together and the larger hook, ch 50. Fasten off, leaving a long tail. This cord will divide the ladybug's wings along the middle of the hat.

Finishing

Find the middle of the hat. Place the cord along the centerline of the hat from brim to brim, going over the top of the hat. Sew it down through the chains, being sure not to sew too tightly, so that the hat stays supple.

Place the ladybug's face so that it hides the end of the cord. Sew the face to the hat along the last round.

Sew the nose to the center of the face.

With the turquoise yarn, embroider two eyes, using the photo as a guide.

Sew the 2 large spots on each side of the cord, approximately 4 rnds from the top of hat.

Sew the other spots around the hat, 2 on each side of the cord.

SANDALS

Sole

(Make 2 in red and 2 in black)

With the red yarn and the larger hook, work rnds 1–5 of the strawberry bootie, join with a sl st and fasten off.

Strap

(Make 2)

With the black yarn and the C-2 (2.75mm) hook, ch 42.

Row 1: Sc in 2nd ch from hook, sc in next

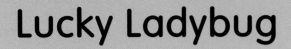

Lucky Ladybug

19 ch, (2 sc) in next ch, sc in next 20 ch, ch 1. Turn.

Row 2: Sc in next 21 sc, (2 sc) in next sc, place marker in first sc made for toe, sc in each sc to end, ch 1. Turn.

Row 3: Sc in next 13 sc, ch 1. Turn.

Row 4: Sc in next 3 sc, ch 1. Turn.

Rows 5–7: Rep row 4. Do not turn at the end of row 7. Working along the side of the last 4 rows, work 5 sc evenly, join with sl st to base of strap, continue in sc to the toe, sc in toe, ch 4 for thong, sl st in 2nd ch from hook, sl st in each ch to the base, join with sl st to toe, sc in next 10 sc, ch 1. Turn.

Rep rows 4–7. Do not turn at the end of row 7. Working along the side of the last 4 rows, work 5 sc evenly, join with sl st to base of strap, sc in each sc to the end of the strap. Fasten off, leaving a long tail. Use the tail to sew the ends of the strap together.

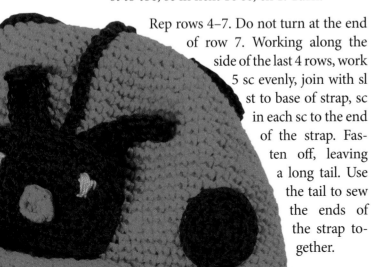

Body for Little Ladybugs

(Make 1 for each sandal)

With the black yarn and the B-1 (2.25mm) hook, ch 7.

Rnd 1: Sc in 2nd ch from hook, sc in each ch to end, (3 sc) in last ch, place marker in center sc, work in opposite side of ch, sc to end, (2 sc) in last ch.

Rnd 2: Sc in each sc to marked st, (3 sc) in marked st, sc to end, (3 sc) in last sc, sc in next st, sl st in next st, ch 1. Turn.

Antennae rnd: Sc in next sc, ch 4, 4 sc in 2nd ch from hook, sl st in each ch to base of ch, sc in next 2 sc, ch 4, sc in 2nd ch from hook, sl st in each ch to base of ch, join with sl st to edge of body. Fasten off, leaving a long tail.

Little Ladybugs' Wings

(Make 2 for each sandal)

With the red yarn and the B-1 (2.25mm) hook, ch 7.

Rnd 1: Sc in 2nd ch from hook, sc in next 4 ch, (5 sc) in last ch, place marker in center sc; working in opposite side of ch, sc in each ch to last ch, ch 2, sl st in 2nd ch from hook.

Rnd 2: Sc in each st to marked st, (4 sc) in marked st, sc in each sc to end, join with sl st. Fasten off, leaving a long tail.

Finishing

Place a red sole on a black sole with the wrong sides together. With the tapestry needle and yarn of any color (you will remove it later) tack them together along the beginning ch.

Matching the center back of the strap to the center of the heel on the red sole, pin the 4-st squares to the soles where they fall, pinning the lower edge of the square between the red and black soles. Sew the thong to the red sole, a few rounds from the edge and slightly to the left of center for the right bootie, slightly to the right for the left bootie.

With the D-3 (3.25mm) hook and the black yarn, starting from the back, work sc around the sole through the sts of the last rnds of the 2 soles together, increasing 3 sts each at the toe and heel, and joining the side squares between the soles when you come to them. Join with a sl st at the end of the rnd and fasten off.

Place the 2 wings, with the tips towards the antennae, above the black oval of the ladybug's body and sew them to the body. Place the ladybug on the thong, with the antennae facing down (see photo), and sew the wings to the strap of the sandal.

With the tapestry needle and the black yarn embroider 3 small dots on each wing. Be sure that the body is securely attached to the sandal.

The Sun Returns and the Mimosa Blooms

A brightly colored pattern that will appeal to every child and—why not?! It celebrates their unique mother.

MATERIALS

For the hat: 3¹/₂oz/100g of cotton fingering yarn in yellow, 1³/₄oz/50g of bright green, sizes B-1, C-2, and D-3 (2.25, 2.75, and 3mm) crochet hooks, tapestry needle, elastic thread, stitch markers.

For the booties: 1³/₄oz/50g of cotton fingering yarn in yellow, 1³/₄oz/50g in bright green, size D-3 (3.25mm) crochet hook, tapestry needle, elastic thread.

… and the Mimosa Blooms

HAT

With the yellow yarn and size D-3 (3.25mm) hook, ch 4, join with sl st to form ring.

Rnd 1: Work 9 sc in ring.

Rnd 2: (2 sc) in each sc around.

Rnd 3: *Sc in next 2 sc, (2 sc) in next sc; rep from * around.

Rnds 4 and 5: *Sc in next 5 sc, (2 sc) in next sc; rep from * around, sc to end if needed.

Rnd 6: *Sc in next 3 sc, (2 sc) in next sc; rep from * around.

Rnd 7: Work Astrakhan st in each sc around. (See box below.)

Rnd 8: *Sc in next 4 sts, (2 sc) in next st; rep from * around.

Rnd 9: Work Astrakhan st in each sc around.

Rnd 10: *Sc in next 5 sts, (2 sc) in next st; rep from * around.

Rnd 11: Work Astrakhan st in each sc around.

Rnd 12: *Sc in next 6 sts, (2 sc) in next st; rep from * around.

Rnd 13: Work Astrakhan st in each sc around.

Rnd 14: *Sc in next 7 sts, (2 sc) in next st; rep from * around.

Rnd 15: Work Astrakhan st in each sc around. Count to be sure you have 72 sts in rnd, inc or dec in rnd 16 if necessary.

Rnd 16: Sc in each st around.

Rnd 17: Work Astrakhan st in each sc around.

ASTRAKHAN STITCH

Keep the yarn taut when working the yarn overs in this stitch. *Insert hook in next sc, yarn over hook and draw through the st (2 loops on hook), ch 5 in yarn over (2 loops on hook), insert hook in same sc, yarn over hook and draw through the sc and both loops on hook—1 Astrakhan st complete.

54

Work 1 rnd in sc, 1 rnd in Astrakhan st until there are 14 total rnds in Astrakhan st.

Next rnd: Sc tightly in each st around.

Brim

Rnd 1: *Sc in next 2 sc; (2 sc) in next sc; rep from * around.

Rnd 2: Sc in each sc around.

Rnd 3: *Sc in next 8 sc, (2 sc) in next sc; rep from * around, sc to end.

Rnd 4–6: Sc in each sc around. Sl st in each sc around. Fasten off.

Leaves

(Make 7)

With the bright green yarn and the C-2 (2.75mm) hook, ch 30.

Rnd 1: Sl st in 2nd ch from hook, sl st in next 9 chs—first cord made. Do not fasten off.

Rnd 2: Ch 13, sl st in 2nd ch, sl st in next 9 chs—cord made.

Rnds 3 and 4: Rep rnd 2.

Rnd 5: Ch 10, sl st in 2nd ch from hook, sl st in each st to beg of the previous cord.

Rnd 6: Ch 10, sl st in 2nd ch from hook, sl st to end.

Rep rnds 2–5 in opposite side of foundation ch. When rnd 5 is complete, sl st to end of beg ch for stem. Fasten off.

Finishing

Thread the stem of one leaf through the center of the hat and weave it towards the outside by threading it into the 1st rnd. Pull it into position and knot tightly. Add the other leaves in the same way.

BOOTIES

With the yellow yarn, work rnds 1–9 as for the strawberry booties.

Rnd 9: Work Astrakhan st in each sc around.

Rnd 10: Work sc in each st around.

Rnd 11: Work Astrakhan st in each sc around.

Rnd 12: Work sc in each st around.

... and the Mimosa Blooms

Rnd 13: Work Astrakhan st in each sc around.

Rnd 14: Sc in next 10 sts, sc2tog, [sc in next 9 sts, sc2tog] twice, sc to last 2 sts, sc2tog.

Fasten off.

Upper

Flatten the bootie lengthwise and find the middle point between the toe of the bootie and the heel, join yarn and ch 8, join with sl st to opposite side.

Row 1: Work Astrakhan st in each ch across, ch 1. Turn.

Row 2: (2 sc) in next st, sc in each st to end (2 sc) in last st, ch 1. Turn.

Row 3: Work Astrakhan st in each sc across, ch 1. Turn.

Row 4: Rep row 2.

Row 5: Rep row 3.

Row 6: Sc in each st across.

Row 7: Rep row 3.

Row 8: Sc2tog, sc to last 2 sts, sc2tog, ch 1. Turn.

Row 9: Rep row 3.

Row 10: Rep row 8. Fasten off.

Make a 2nd bootie same as first.

With the tapestry needle and the yellow yarn, and the wrong side of the bootie facing you, sew the upper in place. Turn the booties right side out.

Leaves

Cut the elastic to the measurement of the cuff of the bootie and join it to the back of the cuff with a knot on the outside of the fabric. With the C-2 (2.75mm) hook, join the green yarn to the same place.

Rnd 1: Holding the elastic and the yarn together, sc, inc 4 sts evenly around.

Rnd 2: *Sc in next sc, ch 10 , sl st in 2nd ch from hook, sl st in each ch, skip next sc, sc in next sc; rep from * around.

Rnd 3: Ch 7, work as for rnd 2, alternating ch 10 and ch 7 to the end of the rnd. Fasten off.

Gently pull the elastic, holding the knot, to gather the leaves slightly.

Ducky Cap

This adorable peaked cap with its matching booties fills the "bill" for a stroll in the park to feed the ducks.

MATERIALS

For the hat: 3½oz/100g of cotton fingering yarn in yellow, small amounts of orange, white, turquoise and black, sizes C-2 and D-3 (2.75 and 3.25mm) crochet hooks, tapestry needle, stitch markers.

For the booties: 1¾oz/50g of cotton fingering yarn in yellow, small amounts of orange, white, turquoise, and black, size D-3 (3.25mm) crochet hook, tapestry needle.

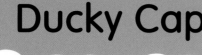

Ducky Cap

HAT

With the yellow yarn and the larger hook, work as for the strawberry hat through rnd 34. Fasten off.

Visor

Row 1: Join the orange yarn with a sl st in the front loop of any sc along the edge of the hat, sc in the front loop of the same st as joining and sc in the front loop of the next 33 sts, ch 1. Turn.

Row 2: Sc in front loop of next 34 sc, ch 1. Turn.

Row 3: Skip 1 st, sc in both loops of each sc to the last st skip last st, ch 1. Turn.

Rows 4–6: Rep rnd 3.

Row 7: Skip 2 sc, sc to last 2 sc, ch 1. Turn.

Rows 8 and 9: Rep rnd 7. Fasten off.

Finishing rnd: Join the orange yarn with a sl st to the back of the hat, sc in same st as joining, sc in each st around, including the edge of the visor, join with a sl st to beg of rnd. Fasten off.

ATTENTION: Work carefully along the edge of the bill, keeping the yarn taut.

Eyes

(Make 2)

With the smaller hook and the turquoise yarn, ch 4.

Rnd 1: Sc in 2nd ch from hook, sc in each ch to end (3 sc) in last ch, place marker in center sc, work in opposite side of ch, sc in each ch to last ch, (3 sc) in last ch, place marker in center sc.

Rnd 2: [Sc in each sc to marker, (3 sc) in marker st, move marker up] twice, sc to end.

Rnd 3: Rep rnd 2, join with sl st. Fasten off.

Rnds 4 and 5: With the white yarn, [sc in each st to marked st, (2 sc) in next 2 sts, move marker up] twice, sc to end.

Fasten off.

Pupils

(Make 2)

With the black yarn and the C-2 (2.75mm) hook, ch 4, join with sl st to form ring.

Rnd 1: Work 8 sc in ring.

Rnd 2: (2 sc) in each sc around.

Rnd 3: *Sc in each sc, (2 sc) in next sc; rep from * around. Fasten off.

Duck's Tuft of Hair

With the black yarn and the smaller hook, ch 20. Sc in 2nd ch from hook, sc in each ch to end, ch 15, sc in 2nd ch from hook, sc in each ch to end, ch 12, sc in 2nd ch from hook, sc in each ch to end. Fasten off.

Finishing

Sew the pupils to the eyes, using photo as a guide.

Sew the eyes to the cap, keeping the yarn loose so that you don't lose the elasticity of the hat.

Sew the black tuft of hair to the top of the hat, leaving the duck's three hairs hanging free on its forehead.

BOOTIES

With the yellow yarn and the size D-3 (3.25mm) hook, work as for the strawberry booties without sewing the upper to the sole.

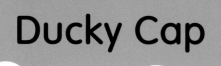

Ducky Cap

Join the orange yarn to the edge of the upper, 5 rnds down from the beginning of the upper. With the smaller hook, sc in each st working towards the toe and around to the opposite side of the upper, ch 1. Turn. Work in reverse sc in each orange sc. Fasten off.

Make a 2nd bootie same as the first.

Eyes for Bootie

(Make 2 for each bootie)

With the turquoise yarn and the smaller hook, ch 4.

Rnd 1: Sc in 2nd ch from hook, (3 sc) in next ch, sc in next ch, (3 sc) in next ch, join with sl st to form ring.

Rnd 2: Continue in the round, (3 sc) in next sc, sc in next 3 sc, (3 sc) in next sc, sc to end, join with a sl st. Fasten off.

Pupils

(Make 2 for each bootie)

With the black yarn and the smaller hook, ch 4, join with sl st to form ring. Work 8 sc in ring, join with sl st. Fasten off.

With 2 strands of black yarn held together and the larger hook, make 2 drawstrings of 60 ch each.

Finishing

Sew the pupils onto the eyes, using the photo as a guide.

Sew the small eyes onto the uppers.

With the yellow yarn, sew the upper to the edge of the bootie, sewing onto the last yellow rnd of the upper and leaving the whole orange portion free.

Insert the drawstring into the cuff, weaving it through the stitches, ending with both ends in the front on the outside. Make a small knot on each end of the drawstring.

63

The Little Rooster

This happy little rooster wakes the household
and is ready to party!

MATERIALS

For the hat: 3½oz/100g of cotton fingering yarn in white, small amounts of red, black and orange, sizes C-2 and D-3 (2.75 and 3.25mm) crochet hooks, tapestry needle, stitch markers.

For the booties: 1¾oz/50g of cotton fingering yarn in white, small amounts of red, black and orange, size D-3 (3.25mm) crochet hook, tapestry needle.

The Little Rooster

HAT

With the larger hook and the white yarn, work as for the frog hat through the brim.

Comb

With the smaller hook and the red yarn, ch 31.

Rnd 1: (2 sc) in 2nd ch from hook, sc in each ch to end, (4 sc) in last ch, work in opposite side of ch, sc in each sc to end, (2 sc) in last ch, join with sl st, ch 1.

Rnd 2: Working over the sts of rnd 1, join with sc in first ch in center of foundation ch, ch 8, sc in 2nd ch from hook, sc in next 2 ch, dc in next ch, tr in next 3 ch, sc in 3rd ch in center of foundation ch, *ch 9, sc in 2nd ch from hook, sc in next 3 ch, dc in next ch, tr in next 3 ch, skip 2 sts of foundation ch, join with sc in next ch; rep from * until all 30 sts in foundation chain have been used. Fasten off.

Beak

With the orange yarn and the smaller hook, ch 6.

Rnd 1: Sc in 2nd ch from hook, sc in each ch to end, (3 sc) in last ch, place marker in center sc, work in opposite side of ch, sc in each ch to end, (2 sc) in last ch, place marker in last sc.

Rnd 2: [Sc in each sc to marked st, (2 sc) in marked st, move marker to last sc] twice, sc to end.

Rnd 3: Rep rnd 2.

Rnd 4: [Sc in each sc to marked st, sc in marked st, ch 2, sl st in base of ch] twice, sc in each sc to end. Fasten off.

Finishing

Flatten the hat to find the center. Pin the comb to the top of the hat, using the photo as a guide. Sew both sides of the comb to the hat, being sure not to make the sts too tight. Tack the center of the beak to the hat.

With the black yarn embroider 2 small eyes, using photo as a guide.

BOOTIES

With the white cotton yarn and the larger hook, make two booties same as the frog booties through the upper.

Comb

(Make 1 for each bootie)

With the red yarn and the smaller hook, ch 9.

Rnd 1: (2 sc) in 2nd ch from hook, sc in each ch to last ch, (4 sc) in last ch, work in opposite side of ch, skip first ch, sc in each ch to end, (2 sc) last ch, join with sl st, ch 1.

Rnd 2: *Sc in first ch in center of foundation ch, ch 6, sl st in 2nd ch from hook, sc in next 2 ch, dc in next ch, tr in next ch, skip next st in foundation ch, join with sc in next st; rep from * until you have 3 points.

Fasten off.

Beak

(Make 1 for each bootie)

With orange yarn and smaller hook, ch 4.

Rnd 1: Sc in 2nd ch from hook, sc in each ch to end, (4 sc) in last ch, place marker in 2nd sc, work in opposite side of ch, sc in each ch to end (3 sc) in last ch, place marker in center sc.

Rnd 2: [Sc in each sc to marked st, sc in marked st, ch 2, sl st in base of ch] twice, sc to end. Fasten off.

Finishing

Using the photo as a guide, sew the combs and beaks to the booties. With tapestry needle and black yarn, embroider eyes on the booties.

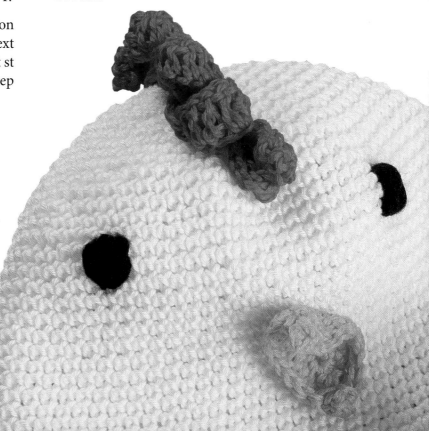

The Busy, Busy Bee

A hat for the child who never stops,
except to smell the flowers.

MATERIALS

For the hat: 3½oz/100g of cotton fingering yarn in in yellow, small amounts of black, red and turquoise, sizes C-2 and D-3 (2.75 and 3.25mm) crochet hooks, tapestry needle, stitch markers.

For the booties: 1¾oz/50g of cotton fingering yarn in yellow, small amounts of black, red and turquoise, sizes C-2 and D-3 (2.75 and 3.25mm) crochet hooks, tapestry needle.

The Busy, Busy Bee

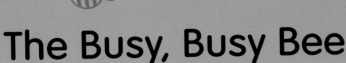

HAT

With the yellow yarn and the larger hook, work rnds 1–19 of strawberry hat.

Rnd 20: Drop the yellow yarn without fastening off, and with the black yarn sc in each sc around.

Rnds 21 and 22: Drop the black yarn, with yellow, sc in each sc around.

Rnds 23 and 24: With black, sc in each sc around.

Rnds 25 and 26: With yellow, sc in each sc around.

Rnds 27 and 28: With black, sc in each sc around.

Rnds 29 and 30: With yellow, sc in each sc around.

Rnd 31: With black, sc in each sc around. Fasten off the black yarn.

Rnds 32–34: With yellow, sc in each sc around. Fasten off the yellow yarn at the end of rnd 34.

Brim

Rnd 1: *Sc in next 3 sc, (2 sc) in next sc; rep from * around.

Rnd 2: Sc in each sc around.

Rnd 3: *Sc in next 8 sc, (2 sc) in next sc; rep from * around.

Rnds 4 and 5: Sc in each sc around.

Rnd 6: Sl st in each st around, holding yarn taut. Fasten off.

Antennae

(Make 2)

With the black yarn and the smaller hook, ch 12.

Rnd 1: Sc in 2nd ch from hook, sc in every ch to end, (2 sc) in last ch, working in opposite side of ch, sc in each ch to end, (5 sc) in last ch.

Rnd 2: Sl st in each sc to end. Fasten off.

Nose

With the red yarn and the smaller hook, ch 4, join with sl st to form ring.

Rnd 1: 8 sc in ring.

Rnd 2: (2 sc) in each sc.

Rnd 3: Sc in each sc.

Rnd 4: *Sc in next sc, skip next sc; rep from * around, join with sl st. Fasten off.

Eyes

(Make 2)

With the turquoise yarn and the smaller hook, ch 5.

Rnd 1: Sc in 2nd ch from hook, sc to last ch, (3 sc) in last ch, working in other side of ch, sc in each ch to end (3 sc) in last ch.

Rnd 2: (2 sc) in next 2 sc, sc in each sc to last 2 sts, (2 sc) in next 2 sc.

Rnd 3: Rep rnd 2.

Rnd 4: Sc in each sc around, join with sl st. Fasten off.

Pupils

(Make 2)

With the black yarn and the smaller hook, ch 3, join with a sl st to form ring.

Rnd 1: 8 sc in ring.

Rnd 2: (2 sc) in each sc.

Rnd 3:
*Sc in
next sc; (2
sc) in next sc;
rep from * around,
join with sl st. Fasten off.

Finishing

Making the color changes the center back of the hat, sew the nose to the center of the front, using the photo as a guide. Then sew on the antennae, each approx 1¼in./3cm from the center. Sew the pupils to the eyes, and sew the eyes to the hat.

BOOTIES

With the yellow yarn and the larger hook, work rnds 1–8 of the strawberry booties.

Rnd 9: Drop the yellow yarn without cutting it and with black, sc in each sc around.

Rnd 10: With yellow, sc in each sc around.

Rnd 11: Rep rnd 9.

Rnd 12: Rep rnd 10. Fasten off the yellow yarn.

Rnd 13: Rep rnd 9. Fasten off.

The Busy, Busy Bee

Upper

With the yellow yarn and the larger hook, work as for Strawberry bootie.

With the black yarn work sc in each sc along the edge of the upper that will be sewn to the bootie. Fasten off.

Cuff

Join the yellow yarn and work in sc, inc 4 sc evenly in rnd, by (2 sc) in same sc 4 times.

Rnds 2–5: Sc in each sc around.

Rnd 6: Work a round of reverse single crochet.

Antennae

(Make 2 for each bootie)

With the black yarn and the smaller hook, ch 7.

Rnd 1: (4 sc) in 2nd ch from hook, sc in each ch to end. Fasten off.

Nose

(Make 1 for each bootie)

With the red yarn and the smaller hook, ch 3, join with sl st to form ring.

Rnd 1: 7 sc in ring.

Rnd 2: Sc in each sc around. Fasten off.

Drawstrings

(Make 1 for each bootie)

With 2 strands of yellow held together and larger hook, ch 60. Fasten off.

Finishing

With the black yarn, sew the upper to the edge of the bootie.

With the tapestry needle, thread the red yarn through the sts of the nose and draw tight to form a ball. Using the photo as a guide, sew the nose to the top of the bootie.

With the tapestry needle and the black yarn, sew the antennae to the bootie, leaving the ends free.

With the tapestry needle and the turquoise yarn, embroider two large eyes, using the photo as a guide.

Weave the two drawstrings into the instep of the bootie between the 2nd and 3rd rnds, leaving the ends free in the front. Knot each end and tie them in a bow.

A Pink Piggy

This adorable pig wouldn't think
of jumping in a mud puddle.

MATERIALS

For the hat: 3¹/₂oz/100g of cotton fingering yarn in pink, and small amounts of acid green and black, sizes C-2 and D-3 (2.75 and 3.25mm) crochet hooks, tapestry needle, stitch markers.

For the booties: 1³/₄oz/50g of cotton fingering yarn in pink, and small amounts of acid green and black, size D-3 (3.25mm) crochet hook, tapestry needle, elastic thread.

A Pink Piggy

With the pink cotton, work as for the frog hat through the brim.

Ears

Fold and flatten the hat and place markers on each side, 16 rnds down from the top.

Row 1: Join the yarn in 1 st at the marker, sc in 7 sts working toward the top of the hat, ch 1. Turn.

Row 2: Sc in each sc, ch 1. Turn.

Row 3: Skip 1 sc, sc in each sc to end, ch 1. Turn. Rep rnd 3 until 1 st remains. Sc along the edge of the ear to the base of the ear, join to the hat with a sl st.

Rep for the 2nd ear at the other marker.

With the acid green yarn and the smaller hook, work in sc around the ears, working (3 sc) in the st on the tip, join with a sl st to the base of the ear. Work 1 row of reverse single crochet along the edge of the ear.

Snout

With the pink yarn and the smaller hook, ch 5.

Rnd 1: Sc in each ch to end, (3 sc) in last ch, place marker in center sc, work in opposite side of ch to last ch, (3 sc) in last ch, place marker in center sc.

Rnd 2: [Sc in each sc half way to marked st, (2 sc) in next sc, sc in each sc to marked st, (3 sc) in marked sc, move marker up] twice, sc to end.

Rnd 3: [Sc in each sc to marked st, (3 sc) in marked st] twice, moving markers up, sc to end.

Rnd 4: Rep rnd 2.

Rnd 5: [Increasing 2 sts evenly spaced, sc to marked st, (3 sc) in marked sc] twice, moving markers up, sc to end.

Rnd 6: Rep rnd 5. Fasten off.

Rnd 7: With the acid green yarn work sc in each sc around. Work 1 rnd in reverse single crochet. Fasten off.

With the tapestry needle and the green yarn, embroider two nostrils, using photo as a guide.

Finishing

Using the photo as a guide, sew the snout on the hat, being sure not to make the stitches too tight to keep the elasticity of the fabric.

With the tapestry needle and the black yarn, embroider two small eyes using photo as a guide.

BOOTIES

Working with the pink yarn, work as for the frog bootie to the upper.

Upper

Row 1: Sc into each of the 8 ch, ch 1. Turn.

Rows 2–6: (2 sc) in next sc, sc to last sc, (2 sc) in last sc, ch 1. Turn.

Row 7: Sc2tog, sc in each sc to last 2 sts, sc2tog, ch 1. Turn.

Row 8: Sc2tog, sc in each sc to last 2 sts, sc2tog. Fasten off.

Row 9: With the acid green yarn, work 1 row of reverse single crochet along the edge of the upper. Fasten off.

Ears

Row 1: With the smaller hook and the pink yarn, work 4 sc in each of 4 sts of the foundation chain for the upper, ch 1. Turn.

Row 2: Sc in each sc, ch 1. Turn.

Row 3: [Sc2tog] twice. Turn.

Row 4: Sc2tog, sc along the edge of the ear, and repeat rnds 1–4 for the other ear.

Join the green yarn to the base of the first ear, sc in each st to the ear tip, ch 2, sl st in base of ch, work in sc to the tip of the 2nd ear, ch 2, sl st in base of ch, work in sc to the base of the 2nd ear. Fasten off.

A Pink Piggy

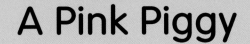

Sew the upper to the edge of the bootie, leaving the green reverse single crochet free.

Make a 2nd bootie same as the first.

Snout

(Make 1 for each bootie)

With the pink yarn and the smaller hook, ch 4.

Rnd 1: (3 sc) in 2nd ch from hook, sc in each ch to last ch, (3 sc) in last ch, place a marker, in center st, work in the opposite side of the ch, sc in each ch to end.

Rnd 2: (2 sc) in next sc, sc in each sc to next marker, (2 sc) in marked st, sc to end.

Rnd 3: Rep rnd 2. Fasten off.

Rnd 4: With the acid green yarn, work 1 rnd reverse single crochet. Fasten off.

With the green yarn and the tapestry needle, embroider 2 small nostrils.

Sew the snout to the bootie and, with the black yarn, embroider 2 small eyes.

Finishing the cuff

Cut the elastic to the measurement of the circumference of the cuff. Knot the end and thread the elastic through the back of the bootie at the edge of the cuff, leaving the knot on the outside.

Rnd 1: Working over the elastic with pink yarn, sc in each sc around.

Rnd 2: *Ch 5, skip 2 sc, sc in next sc; rep from * around. At the end of the rnd, fasten the last ch 5 in the first ch-5 space.

Rnd 3: *Ch 7, sc in ch-5 space; rep from * around. Fasten off. Gently pull the elastic knot to gather the cuff, so that it resembles a small bow. Tighten the knot and cut off the excess elastic.

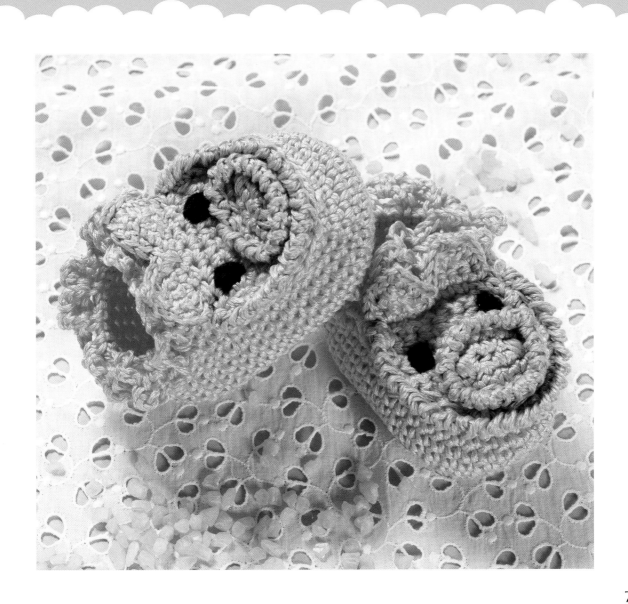

Wise, Wide-eyed Owl!

Wide-eyed with curiousity, your baby will become wise like an owl.

MATERIALS

For the hat: 3¹/₂oz/100g of cotton fingering yarn in pistachio green, small amounts of black, orange and yellow, sizes B-1 and D-3 (2.25 and 3.25mm) crochet hooks, tapestry needle, stitch markers.

For the booties: 1³/₄oz/50g of cotton fingering yarn in pistachio green, small amounts of black, orange and yellow, sizes B-1 and D-3 (2.25 and 3.25mm) crochet hooks, tapestry needle, stitch markers, elastic thread.

Wise, Wide-eyed Owl

HAT

With the green yarn and the larger hook, work as for the frog hat through the brim.

Ears

Flatten the hat and place a marker in each side 16 rnds down from the top.

Row 1: Join the green yarn in 1 st at the marker, sc in 7 sts working toward the top of the hat, ch 1. Turn.

Row 2: Sc2tog, sc in each sc to last 2 sts, sc2tog, ch 1. Turn.

Row 3: Rep rnd 2.

Row 4: Sc3tog, ch 2, sl st in base of ch, sc along edge of ear to base of ear, join to hat with sl st. Fasten off.

Rep in the marked st on the opposite side for the 2nd ear.

Eyes

(Make 2)

With the smaller hook and black yarn, ch 3 join with a sl st to form ring.

Rnd 1: 8 sc in ring.

Rnd 2: *Sc in next sc, (2 sc) in next sc; rep from * around.

Rnd 3: Rep rnd 2.

Rnd 4: *Sc in next 3 sc; (2 sc) in next sc; rep from * around, sc to end.

Rnds 5 and 6: Rep rnd 4. Fasten off.

Rnd 7: With the orange yarn, *sc in next 4 sc, (2 sc) in next sc; rep from * around, sc to end.

Rnd 8: Rep rnd 7. Fasten off.

Rnd 9: With the yellow yarn, rep rnd 7, join with sl st. Fasten off.

Beak

With the orange yarn, ch 4.

Row 1: Sc in each ch to end, ch 1. Turn.

Row 2: Sc2tog, sc to end of row, ch 1. Turn.

Row 3: Sc2tog, work sc around the entire

beak back to the point, ch 2, sl st in base of ch. Fasten off.

Finishing

Flatten the hat to find the best position for the owl's eyes. Sew the eyes to the hat, being careful not to sew too tightly to keep the fabric elastic.

Tack the beak to the hat, using photo as a guide.

SANDALS

With the green yarn, work as for the strawberry bootie through rnd 5. Fasten off.

Make another sole in the same way.

The Front of the Sandal

With the green yarn and the larger hook, ch 13.

Row 1: Sc in 2nd ch from hook and in next 11 sc. Turn.

Row 2: (2 sc) in next sc, sc in next 4 sc, (2 sc) in next sc, sc in next 5 sc, (2 sc) in last sc. Turn.

Row 3: Sc in next 7 sc, (2 sc) in next sc, sc in each sc to end. Turn.

Rows 4–7: Sc in each sc across.

Row 8: Sc in each sc to last st, (3 sc) in last st, work in sc along the side of work to the bottom, (3 sc) in corner, working in the opposite side of the foundation ch, sc in each ch to end, (3 sc) in last ch, sc along side edge to next corner, (3 sc) in corner. Turn.

Ankle Strap

Row 1: Sc in next 5 sc. Turn.

Row 2: Skip next sc, sc in 4 sc, ch 1. Turn.

Rows 3–26: Sc in 4 sc, ch 1. Turn. Fasten off.

Sew the last row of the strap to the other side of the sandal front.

Cuff

Join the orange yarn at the center back of the strap and work around the top edge in sc. Cut the elastic slightly longer than the circumference of cuff and knot the ends. Leaving the knot at the center back of the strap, and working over the elastic, work one round in reverse single crochet. Fasten off.

Wise, Wide-eyed Owl

Rep for the other sandal.

Eyes

(Make 2 for each bootie)

With the black yarn and the C-2 (2.75mm) hook, ch 3, join with a sl st to form ring.

Rnd 1: 8 sc in ring, join with sl st.

Rnd 2: (2 sc) in each sc around, join with sl st. Fasten off.

Rnd 3: Join the orange yarn, *sc in next sc, (2 sc) in next sc; rep from * around. Fasten off.

Beak

(Make 1 for each bootie)

With the yellow yarn and the B-1 (2.25mm) hook, ch 4.

Row 1: 3 sc in the 2nd ch from hook, sc in next 2 ch, ch 2, sl st in base of ch-2, working in opposite side of foundation ch, (2 sc) in next ch, (3 sc) in next ch, (4 sc) in the last ch. Join with sl st and fasten off.

Finishing

Using the photo as a guide, sew the eyes and beak to the front of the sandal.

Sew the sides of the sandal front to the sole along the sc rnd, leaving the reverse single crochet free.

With the D-3 (3.25mm) hook, join the green yarn to the center 6 sts along the back and bottom of the strap, sc in 6 sc, turn. *Sc in 6 sc, turn; rep from * once more. Sew to the corresponding sts of the sole, leaving the reverse single crochet free.

If you would like thicker soles for the sandals, make 2 for each sandal, working to the reverse single crochet rnd, then join them using reverse single crochet. Continue to work the rest of the sandal as instructed.

You can make 2 small flowers in any color you prefer (choose from the models in the first part of the book) and sew them above the owl's eye as in the photo.

Hipster Beanie

A simple, and very elegant hat, perfect
for a day outdoors. A perfect piece
for the most fashionable tot.

MATERIALS

For the hat: 1³/₄oz/50g each of cotton fingering yarn in fuchsia, light pink, and white, small
amounts of purple, size D-3 (3.25mm) crochet hook, tapestry needle, stitch markers.

For the booties: 1³/₄oz/50g each of cotton fingering yarn in fuchsia, light pink, and white, small
amounts of purple, sizes B-1 and D-3 (2.25mm and 3.25mm) crochet hooks, tapestry needle.

Hipster Beanie

HAT

With the white yarn and the D-3 (3.25mm) hook, work as for the strawberry hat through rnd 11.

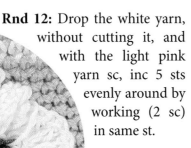

Rnd 12: Drop the white yarn, without cutting it, and with the light pink yarn sc, inc 5 sts evenly around by working (2 sc) in same st.

Rnd 13: Drop the light pink yarn, with the white yarn; working around, sc, inc 7 sts evenly around by working (2 sc) in same st. Fasten off the white yarn.

Rnds 14–24: With the light pink yarn, sc in each sc around.

Rnd 25: Drop light pink, and with the fuchsia yarn, sc in each sc around.

Rnd 26: With light pink yarn, sc in each sc around. Fasten off the light pink yarn.

Rnds 27–33: With fuchsia, sc in each sc around.

Brim

Rnd 1: With fuchsia, *sc in next 3 sc, (2 sc) in next 2 sc; rep from * around, sc to end.

Rnd 2: Sc in each sc around.

Rnd 3: *Sc in next 7 sc, (2 sc) in next sc; rep from * around.

Rnds 4–7: Sc in each sc around. Fasten off.

Rnd 8: With the purple yarn, sl st tightly in each sc around.

Flowers

With the white yarn and the smaller hook, make 3 flowers with 5 petals each (following instructions in the beginning of book), making two of the flowers slightly larger than the third.

Finishing

Sew the flowers to the hat, using the photo as a guide.

With the tapestry needle and the purple yarn, embroider the center of each flower (see photo).

SANDALS

Sole

(Make 2 for each sandal)

With the pink yarn and the larger hook, work rnds 1–6 of the strawberry booties, join with a sl st at the end of rnd 6. Fasten off.

Strap

(Make 1 for each sandal)

With the white yarn and the smaller hook, ch 15.

Row 1: Sc in 2nd ch from hook, sc in each ch to end, ch 1. Turn.

Row 2: (2 sc) in first sc, sc in each sc to last st, (2 sc) in last sc, ch 1. Turn.

Rows 3–5: Sc in each sc across, ch 1. Turn.

Row 6: Sc in each sc across. Fasten off.

Row 7: With the fuchsia yarn, work around the entire edge of the strap in sc, working (3 sc) in same st in each corner, join with sl st. Fasten off.

Sandal Back

Join the white yarn to work on the center 12 sts of the back of 1 sole piece. This is the top sole.

Row 1: Sc in 12 sts, ch 1. Turn.

Rows 2–4: Sc in 12 sc, ch 1. Turn.

Row 5: Sc to last 2 sc, sc2tog, ch 1. Turn.

Rows 6 and 7: Rep rnd 5.

Row 8 (laces): Sc2tog, sc to end, ch 65, sc in 2nd ch from hook, sc in each ch, sc in next 6 sc, ch 65, sc in 2nd ch from hook, sc in each ch. Fasten off.

Side Loops

Join white yarn in 4th st from end of 2nd lace, sc in next 3 sc, ch 1. Turn. Work until

Hipster Beanie

there are 10 rows of 3 sc. Fasten off. Rep at end of other lace.

Rep for 2nd bootie.

Finishing

Pin a top sole to a bottom sole piece with the wrong sides together.

With the purple yarn and the larger hook, begin at the heel, and sc the sole pieces together, joining the strap as you go. Sew

the last round of the side loops to the sole.

Make 6 small fuchsia flowers (3 for each sandal). Sew 3 flowers in a row on the white strap of each sandal.

Embroider a purple center for each flower, taking care to make it big enough to be visible.

Thread the two laces into their respective loops and knot them on the front of the sandal.

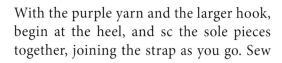

IN FULL COLOR

For a brighter version, work with the colors shown: bright yellow, egg yellow, orange, and red; using purple for the flowers. Work 4 color bands (using the egg yellow and the orange instead of light pink) and make 5 flowers, sewing them in a row. Make the center of the flowers in turquoise for the hat and orange for the sandals. Use yellow for the strap of the sandals, finishing with purple.

Purple is the Color of Eggplant

It's not true that children don't like vegetables, as long as they know the right one to pick!

MATERIALS

For the hat: 3¹/₂oz/100g of cotton fingering yarn in purple, 1³/₄oz/50g of bright green, sizes C-2 and D-3 (2.75 and 3.25mm) crochet hooks, tapestry needle, stitch markers.

For the booties: 1³/₄oz/50g of cotton fingering yarn in purple, small amounts of bright green, sizes C-2 and D-3 (2.75 and 3.25mm) crochet hooks, tapestry needle.

Eggplant

HAT

With the purple yarn and the larger hook, Work as for the frog hat through the brim.

Eggplant's Stem and Leaves

With 2 strands of green held together and the smaller hook, ch 10.

Stem Row: Sc in 2nd ch from hook, sc in each ch to last ch, cut 1 strand and continue with 1 strand only, (6 sc) in last ch, holding the stem to the front, join with sl st to form ring of these 6 sc.

Rnd 1: Sc in each sc.

Rnd 2: (2 sc) in each sc in ring—12 sc.

Rnd 3: *Sc in next 3 sc, (2 sc) in next sc; rep from * around—15 sc.

Rnds 4: *Sc in nex 4 sc, (2 sc) in next sc; rep from * around—18 sc.

Rnds 5–8: Sc around, increasing 3 sc evenly spaced—30 sc.

Rnd 9: *Sc in 9 sc, (2 dc) in next sc, place a marker between the 2 dc; rep from * twice more.

Rnd 10: *Sc in each st to marker, sl st between the 2 dc, ch 9, sc in 2nd ch from hook and in next 2 ch, dc in next 3 ch, tr in next 2 ch, skip next 3 sts; rep from * twice more.

Rnd 11: *Sc to 2 sts before ch, working up opposite side of ch, tr in 2 ch, dc in 3 ch, sc in 3 ch, ch 3, sl st in 2nd ch from hook, sc in each st of leaf; rep from * twice more. Join and fasten off.

Finishing

Sew the eggplant's leaves to the center top of the hat. Sew loosely and leave the tips free, allowing them to curl.

Add some small flowers, a four-leaf clover, a caterpillar, or a yellow ladybug: it's your choice!

BOOTIES

With the purple yarn and the larger hook, work as for the strawberry booties, working only 3 rnds for the cuff, increasing as needed to end with 30 sts.

Leaves

With the green yarn and the smaller hook and the wrong side facing you, start at the front of the cuff, beginning in the stitches that correspond to the ch-8 that divides the cuff from the upper, *sc in next 9 sc, ch 6, sc in 2nd from hook, sc in next ch, dc in next ch, tr in last 2 ch, skip one st; rep from * twice more.

Rnd 2: *Sc to 2 sts before ch, working in opposite side of ch 6, tr in next 2 ch, dc in next ch, sc in next ch, (2 sc) in last ch, sc in each st to base of lear; rep from * twice more.

Last rnd: Sl st in each st around, working the tip of each leaf as follows: ch 3, sl st in st at base of ch, continue around.

Drawstrings

(Make 2)

With 2 strands of purple held together and the larger hook, ch 60, fasten off.

Button

(Make 2)

With the green yarn and the larger hook, ch 4, join with sl st to form ring. Work 9 sc in ring. Fasten off.

Finishing

Sew the upper to the bootie.

Weave the drawstring through the stitches around the ankle so that the ends are on the front on the outside thread the 2 ends through the center of the button. Knot the ends of the drawstring. Use the button to tighten and loosen the cuff.

Puss... in Booties

This set will inspire baby to be
the hero of any fairy tale.

MATERIALS

For the hat: 3¹/₂oz/100g of cotton fingering yarn in orange, small amounts of turquoise and
black, size D-3 (3.25mm) crochet hook, pieces of black raffia, tapestry needle, stitch markers.

For the booties: 1³/₄oz/50g of cotton fingering yarn in orange, size D-3 (3.25mm)
crochet hook, tapestry needle.

Puss… in Booties

HAT

With the orange yarn, work as for the frog hat through the brim.

Ears

Flatten the hat and place markers 15 rows down from the beginning on each side.

Row 1: Join the orange yarn in 1 marked st, working toward the top of the hat, work 5 sc, ch 1. Turn.

Row 2: Sc in each sc across, ch 1. Turn.

Rnds 3 and 4: Sc2tog, sc to end of row, ch 1. Turn.

Rnd 5: Sc2tog, continue in sc along the edge of the ear, sl st to the hat.

Rep at the other marked st for the 2nd ear.

With the turquoise yarn, work 1 row sc along the edge of the ear, join with a sl st, turn and work 1 row of reverse single crochet.

Nose

With the turquoise yarn, ch 4, join with sl st to form ring. Work 8 sc in ring, join with sl st. Fasten off.

Finishing

Sew the nose to the center of the hat, using the photo as a guide.

Using the same yarn, embroider the cat's mouth with chain stitches. Do not cut the yarn.

Cut 10 pieces of raffia, each about 6in./15cm long for the cat's whiskers. Use the crochet hook to help you weave the raffia behind the nose. Sew in place on the wrong side with the turquoise yarn.

Using the tapestry needle and the turquoise yarn, fasten the cat's whiskers on the inside of the hat.

With the black yarn and the tapestry needle embroider the cat's eyes, large enough that they are easy to see.

If desired, make a small flower in your preferred color and weave the stem through the sts, over one eye.

BOOTIES

Work as for the frog booties, but without making the cuff.

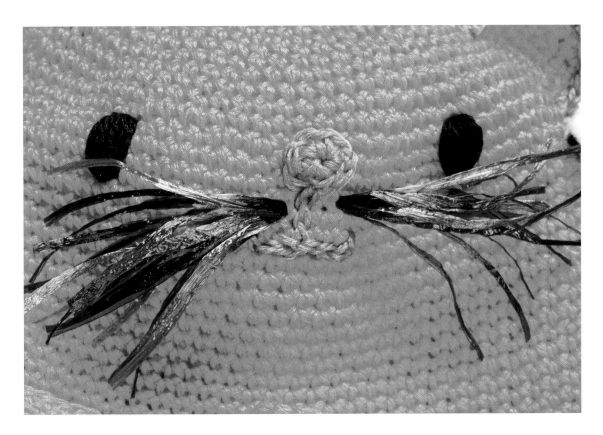

Ears

With the orange yarn and the larger hook, start working in the opposite side of the ch-8 that begins the upper.

Row 1: Sc in next 4 sts. Turn.

Row 2: Sc2tog, sc in next 2 sc. Turn.

Row 3: Sc2tog. Work in sc along the side of the ear, at the base of the ear,* (2 sc) in next sc, sc in next 3 sc. Rep rows 1–3 end at *, join with a sl st. Fasten off.

Puss... in Booties

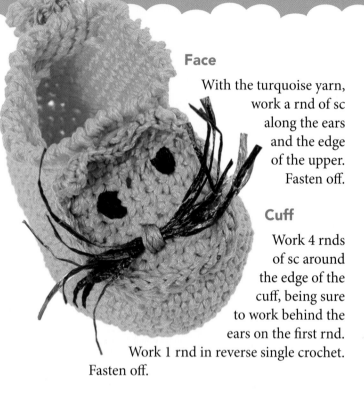

Face

With the turquoise yarn, work a rnd of sc along the ears and the edge of the upper. Fasten off.

Cuff

Work 4 rnds of sc around the edge of the cuff, being sure to work behind the ears on the first rnd. Work 1 rnd in reverse single crochet. Fasten off.

Drawstrings

(Make 2)

With 2 strands of orange yarn held together and the larger hook, ch 60. Fasten off.

Buttons

(Make 2)

With the turquoise yarn ch 4, join with a sl st to form a ring. Work 9 sc in ring. Fasten off.

Finishing

With the tapestry needle and the orange yarn, sew the upper to the sole, leaving the turquoise rnd free. Embroider the eyes and nose on the bootie, using the photo as a guide.

With the raffia, make the whiskers (just like those on the hat, but shorter), pass them under the nose and secure the whiskers on the inside of the bootie with the tail of turquoise yarn.

Thread the drawstrings through the stitches around the cuff so they finish with the ends on the outside on the front.

Thread the ends of the drawstring into the center of the button, which will serve to tighten and loosen the bootie. Knot the ends of the drawstrings

City Mouse or Country Mouse?

Does your little mouse prefer a walk on a city street or a ramble on a country road?

MATERIALS

For the hat: 3½oz/100g of cotton fingering yarn in turquoise and small amounts of orange, size D-3 (3.25mm) crochet hook, small amount of black raffia, tapestry needle, stitch markers.

For the booties: 1¾oz/50g of cotton fingering yarn in turquoise and small amounts of orange, size D-3 (3.25mm) crochet hook, a few pieces of raffia, elastic thread, tapestry needle.

City Mouse or Country Mouse?

HAT

With the turquoise yarn, work as for the frog hat through the brim. Flatten the hat and place a marker on each side, 14 rnds down from the top, for the ears.

Ears

Row 1: Join yarn with a sl st in the marked st, sc in 5 sts working toward the top of the hat. Turn.

Row 2: (2 sc) in next sc, sc in each sc to last st, (2 sc) in last sc. Turn.

Row 3: (2 sc) in next sc, sc in next 2 sc, (2 sc) in next sc, sc in next 2 sc, (2 sc) in last sc. Turn.

Rows 4 and 5: Rep rnd 2. Turn.

Rows 6 and 7: Sc in each sc across. Turn.

Rows 8 and 9: Sc2tog, sc to last 2 sc, sc2tog. Turn. Do not turn at the end of row 9, but continue in sc on the outer edge of the ear, working in every other row of the edge; join with sl st to the hat. Turn and sc along entire edge of ear, working in every other row on the other side; join with sl st. Fasten off.

Work the other ear in the same way starting at the other marked st.

Nose

With the orange yarn, ch 4, join with sl st to form ring. 8 sc in ring. Fasten off, leaving a long tail.

Thread the tail through the tapestry needle and weave the tail through the sts to form a ball.

Finishing

Using the photos as a guide, sew the nose onto the hat and embroider a small mouth and 2 eyes.

Cut 8 pieces of raffia approximately 6in./ 15cm long. Use the crochet hook to help weave the bundle under the nose. Secure the raffia on the wrong side with the tail of the yarn from the nose.

BOOTIES

With the turquoise yarn, work as for the strawberry booties to the upper, without fastening off.

Sc to the middle of one of the sides of the bootie, ch 1. Turn.

Row 1: Sc in next 25 sc (this will be the front of the bootie). Turn.

Rows 2–4: Rep row 1.

Flatten the bootie lengthwise and, with the tapestry needle and the turquoise tail of yarn, sew the sides of the front to the bootie.

Cuff

Join the turquoise yarn at the center of the back of the bootie.

Rnd 1: Sc in each st around the opening of the bootie to form the cuff.

Rnd 2: Sc in each sc around.

Rnd 3: Cut a length of elastic slightly longer than the circumference of the cuff. Knot

City Mouse or Country Mouse?

the end. Keeping the knot on the outside of the bootie, sc in each sc around, working over the elastic.

Rnd 4: Sc in each sc around, inc 6 sts evenly by (2 sc) in same st.

Rnds 5 and 6: Sc in each sc around.

Rnd 7: Sl st tightly in each st around. Fasten off.

Ears

(Make 2 for each bootie)

With the orange yarn, ch 6.

Row 1: Sc in 2nd ch from hook and next 4 ch. Turn.

Row 2: (2 sc) in next sc, sc in next 3 sc, (2 sc) in next sc. Turn.

Row 3: Sc in next 3 sc, (2 sc) in next sc, sc in next 3 sc. Turn.

Row 4: Sc in each sc across. Turn.

Row 5: Sc2tog, sc in next 3 sc, sc2tog. Turn.

Row 6: Sc2tog, sc in each st along edge of ear, join with sl st, turn and work in sc along the edge of the ear to the other side, working in every other row on the sides, join with sl st. Fasten off.

Row 7: Join the orange yarn to one end of ear, work in sc along outer edge. Fasten off.

Finishing

Using the photo as a guide, sew the ears to the bootie.

With the orange yarn and the tapestry needle, embroider 2 small eyes for each mouse.

Make a small bunch of 6–7 pieces of raffia and weave the bunch into the toe of the bootie as for the hat.

With the orange yarn and the tapestry needle, embroider the mouse's nose on the tip of the toe. Secure the whiskers at the inside of the bootie and trim.